D0313623

How to Care for Your Rabbit

CONTENTS

Introduction 4
History 5
Selection 8
Care 17
Health 24
Breeding 28
Conclusion 32
Bibliography 34

We would like to thank the following for permission to photograph their stock: **Hansards Pet Centre, Romsey**

Photos by: **Frank Naylor, Colin Jeal**

KINGDOM

INTRODUCTION

Peter Rabbit, Peter Cottontail, Thumper, Brer Rabbit, Bugs Bunny... Who at some time in their life hasn't listened with delight to a story about one of the many famous rabbits that have captured the imagination of children and grown-ups the world over? And how many youngsters have searched through the house, hunting for those marvellous eggs and gaily-coloured baskets of goodies left by the most famous of all rabbits - the Easter Bunny?

The tales and legends of all these famous rabbits were inspired by an extraordinary, yet everyday, little animal whose great appeal makes it one of the finest pets around. A rabbit, in fact, may be just the kind of pet you are looking for. Being a rather compact creature, it requires little in the way of space and it can make a fine indoor, as well as outdoor, pet.

Lunching as it does chiefly on grains and greens, the rabbit is amazingly inexpensive to keep. To take care of it is not difficult; it is one of the cleanest animals alive - even a white bunny stays snowy white with little help from anyone. A rabbit, being gentle by nature, will warm to you quickly, so don't be surprised when your lap becomes its favourite resting place.

Quick-witted and affectionate, the rabbit has become a popular pet in big cities and in small towns. The rabbit does not require as much time and care as do many other kinds of domesticated pets, yet it has a lot to offer. The rabbit is indeed a likeable little animal which has gathered a faithful following throughout the land. To top all the other desirable characteristics, it makes little noise to disturb the neighbours.

This Agouti French Lop shows off the length of its ears.

4

HISTORY

The rabbit, looking much as it does today, existed long before the dawn of recorded history. It was not until about 1000 BC, however, that it actually got a written mention from the Phoenician traders of the Mediterranean. On their journeys to what is now Spain, these sea-going merchants noticed the abundance of a timid little animal that lived in burrows. In the course of their voyages they transported some of these unknown animals to other parts of Europe and soon the rabbit became a common sight in most of the Mediterranean lands. From there it began to spread out in all directions.

The Romans proved industrious in containing their rabbit 'herds' - stone walls were erected to confine these prolific and intriguing animals. They were impressed by the propagation of the rabbit and believed that its flesh brought beauty and fertility to women.

Rabbits As Pets

It appears that domesticated rabbits were being raised as pets in a few monasteries in France somewhere around the sixth century. It was not until the sixteenth century, however, that rabbits began to be accepted as pets. During more recent times, especially the last several decades, rabbits have really come into their own. Today, without doubt, they can be included among the most popular of pet animals.

There are many varieties of rabbit from which to choose.

The British Rabbit Council and National Rabbit Club are dedicated to the highest standards of rabbit keeping and have worked diligently to foster the development of many breeds of rabbit. Additionally, they have been notably successful in their efforts to educate and inform rabbit keepers who are new to the hobby.

Classification

Due to their long incisor teeth, many people think that rabbits belong to the scientific order that includes mice, hamsters, gerbils and other rodents. However, rabbits differ from these animals in that they have two pairs of incisors, placed one behind the other. This characteristic puts them in the scientific order called Lagomorpha, which also includes pikas and hares. It is from the species *Oryctolagus cuniculus* that all present-day domestic varieties of rabbit in their many different sizes, shapes and colours were developed.

A white Dwarf Lop - the pink eyes are common to this colour.

A Chinchilla Giganta buck aged 12 weeks. When adult he may weigh as much as 5kg.

SELECTION

Many of the names given to rabbits, such as Dutch and Himalayan, are quite exotic. However, these names usually have no connection with the rabbit's real home, for all the tame rabbits around today are descended from those early wild ones of Europe. There are rabbits as big as spaniels; there are rabbits as small as guinea pigs. In between, there are rabbits of every size, shape and colour - more than 50 domestic breeds from which to choose your pet. If this figure overwhelms you, find out from a pet shop or breeder the best breed for you. Although it is not possible to present here every rabbit breed that is available, the following descriptions give the reader a thorough overview of some of the types of rabbit that are available to the hobbyist.

Dutch: This rabbit is coloured similarly fore and aft, with a broad band of white around the front part of its body up to the head. A small-to-medium character with a charming disposition, it comes in a variety of attractive colours. It is no wonder that it has become popular as a pet.

Polish: This is the original dwarf rabbit, a small, lean individual weighing no more than 0.9kg. It is the same size as the more common Netherland Dwarf but the complete opposite in body shape, having a long, graceful body and a racy, alert appearance. The most usual variety is the red-eyed white, although many other colours exist such as black, blue, smoke and sable. The fur of the Polish is very short and shiny, as though it has been polished - hence the name (although 'Polish' is pronounced as if it was derived from Poland). Unfortunately the Polish has a reputation for being bad tempered and is therefore not a pet for the novice.

Belgian Hare: One of the most intelligent of rabbits. This attractive animal, whose weight can range from 2.7kg to 4.5kg, has beautiful lush fur that is reddish tan in colour. Its body shape is similar to that of a hare, with very long legs and ears.

The English has distinct, even spots down each flank.

8

Himalayan: This red-eyed rabbit sports a white coat with black, blue, chocolate or lilac markings. These markings are on the nose, ears, tail, feet and legs. Medium in size, it weighs from 0.9kg to 1.8kg.

Angora: These beautiful rabbits are easily recognisable by the distinctive quality of their coats. This breed is available in white and various other colours. The Angora is more difficult to take care of than some other types of rabbit, but if you devote the necessary time and patience to brushing, cleaning and clipping it you will be rewarded by the beauty of this prized and unusual pet.

Lop: The hallmark of lop rabbits is their long, soft, drooping or 'lop' ears (which in some breeds are enormous in relation to their body size). In the larger lop breeds, ear lengths easily measure over 50cm. The French Lop is the largest variety, growing as big as 6.8kg. It has a very round, compact body shape. The slightly smaller English Lop is a mean, lean shape, with the largest ears of any rabbit. The German Lop, the Dwarf Lop and the Mini Lop are all smaller versions of the French Lop, the Mini Lop being the smallest at approximately 1.4kg. The Meissner Lop has distinctive silver colouring, similar to the silver rabbit, and the Cashmere Lop is the longhaired version of the Dwarf Lop. All Lops come in a great variety of colours and markings, and make excellent pets.

Silver: These beautiful rabbits are the choice of quite a few hobbyists. Silvers, whose coats are short and even in length, are available in several colours, all of which are highlighted by the breed's characteristic silvering. Adult members of the breed weigh from 1.8kg to 3kg.

Netherland Dwarf: These rabbits, often simply called dwarf rabbits, are a favourite of many in the fancy. Their appearance is distinctive: short ears perched on top of an apple-round head, and a very compact body. Netherland Dwarfs, which come in a variety of beautiful colours, are known for their even dispositions.

Chinchilla and Chinchilla Giganta: These are two recognised breeds and are similar in appearance. The Giganta is larger, weighing about 4.9kg to 5kg while the Chinchilla weighs 2.7kg. The distinguishing characteristic of both is the unique colour, 'to resemble real chinchilla'. The undercolour is dark slate blue at the base, light pearl at the centre, and the top banded in black; the chinchilla effect is produced by a very light band brightly ticked with jet black hairs in a wavy fashion. The top colour of the Chinchilla Giganta is darker than the Chinchilla.

A Dutch enjoying some free time in the garden.

The Argente has been recognised for some time but is still relatively rare.

English: In an attractive array of colours, the English comes to modern-day fanciers from a long line of British-bred rabbits, with earliest references dating from the mid-nineteenth century. This racy rabbit is streaked with distinctive markings, which run deep toward the skin. Its features include the butterfly nose, the wing hovering over the whisker beds, and the herringbone spine markings, clearly traceable and unblotched. Its hallmark, however, is the chain of spots along each side of the flanks. The markings on each side should match. In a faultless specimen, the spots are distinct, separate and gracefully sweeping.

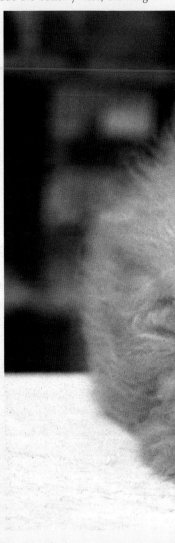

Normal Havana: A furry Dutch rabbit, once dubbed the beaver, the Havana has been a well-known European breed since the turn of the century, exhibited widely in France, Switzerland, Germany, Holland and England. Its present name derives from the brown variety's close colour resemblance to the Cuban cigar. Short, cobby and wholly romantic, the Havana has dark eyes that twinkle a rich ruby glow in a darkened room. The fur is approximately 2.5cm in length.

Flemish Giant: This is a long and powerful rabbit with a notably square and wide body. Colour, which is always uniform, can be any solid except white. As its name suggests, this rabbit blossomed in Flanders, Belgium, where it was known as the Patagonian and favoured for its tremendous size. Its coat is strikingly full and bright, and always of one length.

Californian: A pure white rabbit with black Himalayan markings on the body, this is a 'Roaring Twenties' rabbit creation, achieved by crossing a Himalayan and a Chinchilla. The body is medium long, appearing full and somewhat rounded.

Beveren: Beveren is a small town in Belgium where this rabbit was first bred in the early 1900s. Its initial popularity in England was with butchers, as opposed to pet shop keepers, as meat was very scarce during the First World War. The Beveren's body is shaped like a mandolin and it enjoys being stroked. Considered one of the largest of the fur breeds, the Beveren can weigh up to 4.5kg.

The Angora rabbit requires dedicated coat care.

Rex: Differing from the normal furred rabbits, the Rex varieties exhibit a soft velvety coat achieved by guard hairs of equal length to the undercoat fur. The whiskers on all varieties are curly and fairly short. Originally considered runts in normal-furred litters, the Rex eventually secured mutant status and began to be exhibited as a true breeding oddity, not merely a half-furred outcast. Among the many Rex colours are opal, lynx, sable, seal, blue, castor and chinchilla. Colours often suffer from the lack of density of the coat. There is also a miniature version of the Rex. At only 1.4kg in weight, these rabbits are ideal pets.

Sable: This medium sized rabbit is a well-furred, good-eared little darling who sports a very rich sepia-brown colour, which extends as deep as possible. The eyes are brown with a distinct ruby glow.

Where To Buy

Depending on the breed and colour of your preferred rabbit, you may find it difficult to locate a top-class specimen in your area. Never compromise and take home a sickly animal or a representative of a breed that you don't really like. Remember that happiness with a pet is a mutual thing - you are responsible for looking after the animal for the duration of its life. Adult animals are less likely to be adopted should you decide that you are not compatible or become discontented with your furry charge.

For all the rare and pure breeds, your local rabbit club is your best source. Information about local breeders can be obtained from the BRC. Your local pet shop is ideal for a pet breed. Apply strict criteria to any establishment that is selling live animals. Demand overall cleanliness in the surroundings; look for alert and healthy rabbits and insist upon intelligent answers to all your questions from the staff. A shabby, untidy operation is unlikely to be indicative of good health and hardiness in the stock.

Always know as much as possible before purchasing a pet: be aware of what a healthy specimen looks like, how large a six-week-old rabbit should be, what characteristics are important in your chosen breed, and so on. If you are looking for a particular breed or a less popular colour variety of a known breed, a breeder may be your only possible source of supply. Breeders generally are dedicated and highly knowledgeable fanciers; they are also interested in you and the kind of environment and home you intend to give your new pet.

All Rabbits Are Lovable

After you familiarise yourself with all the rabbit breeds available to hobbyists, you will no doubt give consideration to the question, 'Which one is best for me?' All rabbits are equally lovable and all have their own particular appeal. Probably your decision will be influenced by the rabbit that has 'that special something'. Your most important concern, however, should be to select a rabbit that is healthy and sound.

Best Age To Buy

The best age to buy a rabbit is when it is aged five to eight weeks old. Carefully observe the rabbit you intend to buy. Its eyes should be bright and clear. Its nose should not be runny. It is better not to choose a rabbit with sniffles or sneezes. The coat should be sleek and evenly distributed. Stains or discolourations around the vent could indicate diarrhoea - a sure reason for rejection. Whether to buy a male (a buck) or female (a doe) depends on the buyer. If you buy a female you may wish to breed from her later, and the experience of helping to raise a batch of bunnies is a memorable one. Keep in mind, however, that to care properly for your rabbit family will require considerable time and energy.

Handling

When you first get your new rabbit, you will probably want to hold it. This is very natural since it is one of the most cuddly of all pets. Happily, handling a rabbit makes it even more tame and friendly. Make sure that you are doing it correctly. If your rabbit is still a baby, pick it up with both hands. Slip one hand under the chest, and use the other to support the hindquarters. When the rabbit has grown older, use one hand to hold the loose skin over the shoulders and pick it up with the other hand under the rump. Never pick up a rabbit by the ears.

The Silver Fox - this is Black - can also be found in Blue and Chocolate.

Your new rabbit is like a new baby and should be treated as such. It is best not to handle it too much when you first get it home or invite lots of friends to see it. You will be tempted to do this because you'll want to show off your new pet but this should be done gradually as it becomes more accustomed to having people around it.

You must explain to small children that your rabbit is different from the soft toys they throw around their rooms or pick up by the ears or tail. Show them the proper way to handle it. A rabbit handled incorrectly may kick with its strong hindlegs and cause injury. Never let a child younger than six carry a rabbit - put the rabbit on the child's lap instead. Follow these rules and the rabbit's introduction to your home will be a happy one.

A baby rabbit, like this Rex, needs to be handled gently so that it becomes tame.

Once your new rabbit has settled down you will want to try hard to make it happy. But, when it comes to food, you must temper your affections. The rabbit must be kept on a proper diet which you must try hard to follow. A rabbit fed with the wrong food, or even fed too much of the right food, will become obese, unhappy and unhealthy. Just because a little of something is good, it does not follow that twice as much is even better!

The butterfly nose markings are very clear on this French Lop.

Feeding Guidelines

Do not overfeed your pet. Twice a day, morning and evening, is enough. A good quality rabbit mix, available at your pet shop, should form the mainstay of your pet's diet. This food provides a convenient balanced diet and is used successfully by numerous rabbit keepers. You can supplement the prepared food with an occasional nibble of stale bread. Greens should be offered on a limited basis only, and be sure that any fresh food items are thoroughly washed before they are served to your pet. Some hobbyists like to provide their rabbits with a salt lick or spool, while others feel that prepared rabbit food contains a sufficient amount of this ingredient.

Avoid giving the rabbit leftovers or in-between-meal snacks. You should not, of course, give it meat. Your rabbit is a committed vegetarian! Make sure that plenty of fresh water is available at all times. It is best to serve your rabbit's water in a water bottle attached to the side of the hutch. In this way the water cannot become soiled by droppings or bedding material. Feeding dishes should be deep and heavy so that your pet cannot tip them over.

Acclimatisation

There is more to feeding and taking care of a rabbit than meets the eye. Don't just set the food in front of it and walk away; try to keep it company. Speak to it in a gentle voice, show that you are friendly. When you want the rabbit to come to you, call it by name softly - don't shout. Reward it when it comes to you; eventually it will grow more friendly. As you stroke it, move your hand in the same direction as the lie of the fur - don't ruffle it. Rabbits generally get along well with other pets. However, exercise caution when making introductions. Do not give your other pets any opportunity to harm the rabbit. Some rabbit-keepers claim it's quite a sight to see a rabbit playing with a large dog, even leaping exuberantly over its big friend. Such behaviour, however, is more the exception than the rule.

Housing

Your rabbit needs a good quality wooden rabbit hutch to live in. These are available from pet shops and from specialist hutch manufacturers and come in a wide range of sizes and designs. The hutch should be large enough to allow the rabbit to exercise; at least 150cm wide, 70cm high and 60cm deep. It should be divided into two parts: two-thirds of it a screened-in 'front garden', one-third a secure bedroom. A rabbit demands privacy for sleeping and breeding. Therefore, the bedroom should be enclosed. A flap of burlap provides a simple door and protects your pet from draughts.

The hutch can be in or out of doors but it will require more weatherproofing if kept outside. If you decide to keep the hutch outdoors, place it in a spot that gets some sun but remember to avoid direct sun which will make the hutch too hot. Your rabbit doesn't require much heat but does need a lot of sunlight. The hutch should be built at least 0.6m off the ground, with a sloping roof and a slight overhang; rain will then run off the back. For added protection, canvas flaps can be attached to all four sides and lowered when the weather is bad.

The roof should be hinged to permit easy cleaning. The 'front garden' should be enclosed in one centimetre wire mesh screen; this not only makes the cage mouse-proof, it prevents stray cats from poking their claws through. For bedding, use a material that is soft. Hay is one choice; straw and wood shavings can also be used.

Housekeeping

Whatever material you choose for your rabbit's bedding it should always be clean. Replace the bedding two or three times weekly, except during breeding or after the birth of baby rabbits. Rabbits are among the cleanest animals in the world and they always assist their owners in keeping their home clean and neat. Your pet will usually dirty only one corner of its hutch. Try to clean this corner every day.

Look at the difference between this 4-week-old Chinchilla Giganta and his older relation on page 7.

The entire living area should be cleaned thoroughly at least once a week. Scrub it with a solution of mild disinfectant. Cleanliness is the best insurance for the health of your rabbit. You are lucky to have a pet that is so clean by nature and so easy to care for. Help it along with the aid of these few simple guidelines and you will contribute greatly to its happy and healthy life.

This Black Dutch has everything it needs - a secure home, water and lots of bedding.

Exercise

Rabbits are traditionally lean but this is because they get plenty of exercise in the wild. Domestic rabbits should get as much exercise as possible to prevent them getting fat. If the hutch is big enough, your pet can get much of its exercise just running and hopping about. It is better, however, to take the rabbit out of its quarters as much as possible. A fenced-in garden can make a fine rabbit playground; just remember that your pet should be under supervision at all times. Never let it out in cold or wet weather, as it might get a chill.

Some rabbit owners take their pets out for walks, but I would not advise this as the rabbits could catch diseases from other animals they meet. You can also give the rabbit the run of the house. Be sure to provide a plastic tray of cat litter in a central location. Put some of your pet's droppings in the litter tray to attract its attention and take it to the tray regularly. Hopefully, it will catch on.

Safety Tips

Naturally, you will want to take every step to ensure your rabbit's safety and well-being, both indoors and outdoors. Periodically check your pet's housing for signs of wear-and-tear. A protruding piece of cage wire can cause a painful scratch if your pet brushes against it. By the same token, worn-out materials can become a virtual haven for parasites and other pests.

Food utensils, particularly the feeding dishes, should be heavy in weight to prevent tipping; a lightweight glass or ceramic dish can be shoved about and shattered by a rabbit's vigorous hopping movements.

When you let your pet out of its hutch for playtime and exercise make sure that you are nearby to keep an eye on it. Remember that rabbits love to gnaw and they are not always discriminating in the object of this favourite pastime: chewing on an electrical cord indoors or a toxic object outdoors can lead to quick and unnecessary death.

Poisonous Plants

Contrary to a commonly held assumption, rabbits do not always reject poisonous plants. If your pet is allowed outdoors, you should familiarise yourself with the wild plants that grow in your neighbourhood. Plants to be avoided include foxglove, yew, creeping buttercup, and all plants from bulbs. As a general rule, do not let your pet eat unknown plant matter.

Californian Satins showing characteristic markings inherited from their Himalayan ancestors.

A Himalayan (compare this with the photo opposite).

HEALTH

If you give your rabbit proper care and attention, hopefully it will remain healthy. Most diseases result from the lack of proper care, unsanitary living conditions, bad ventilation, or too much/too little/ improper food. If your rabbit does not respond to the treatments suggested here, call the veterinary surgeon.

Snuffles: Correctly known as contagious rhinitis. Symptoms are a runny nose and sneezing. The nasal discharge can become thick and yellow as the disease progresses. Kept warm and dry, rabbits frequently recover by themselves. In severe cases, the use of sulfa, penicillin or one of the 'mycin' antibiotics is usually effective.

Constipation: A warm mash of boiled potatoes with the skins left on, or clover leaves mixed with bran, can help to alleviate this condition. A modest increase in the amount of greens that you feed to your pet may also help. Clean fresh water should always be available.

Diarrhoea: Immediately eliminate the greens in the diet and increase dry food. Sometimes a little drained boiled rice does wonders for the sufferer.

Canker: This ear ailment is sometimes not noticeable externally. If your pet is shaking its head constantly or scratching at its ears, or if you notice any signs of inflammation, it should be examined for canker. Signs of canker include reddish inflamed areas and crusty legions. For treatment, begin by wiping out the ears with hydrogen peroxide applied with a

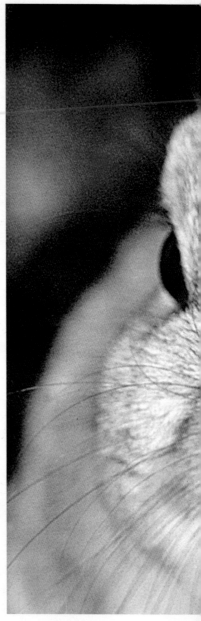

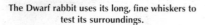
The Dwarf rabbit uses its long, fine whiskers to test its surroundings.

cotton-tipped swab. Afterwards, dust the ear with an appropriate antibiotic. Avoid using preparations that are formulated for dogs. If you are uncertain about selecting the right medication, consult your vet.

Fleas: Like all animals with fur coats, rabbits get fleas. The best way to get rid of them is to use an insecticidal preparation, available from a veterinary surgery or pet shop. Make sure that none gets into the rabbit's eyes. Additionally, clean and treat the hutch thoroughly and change the bedding.

Eye infections: Domestic rabbits are rather susceptible to eye problems, primarily infections caused by dust and/or other flying matter that accumulates in the tear ducts. As a result of the blockage caused by the dirt, fluid fills the eye pocket and subsequently flows down the rabbit's cheeks. What owner can bear to watch his pet weeping? Prevention of dust accumulation should be stressed, as a cure is never as easy as prevention. Often only one eye is affected, although some unfortunate rabbits suffer an infection in both eyes. Eye baths, prescribed by a vet, are frequently required to treat the infection. The skin and fur around the eyes, likewise, may be affected. Draughts may also be responsible for eye infections.

Pneumonia: A rabbit well cared for and properly fed rarely encounters this serious illness. Keep the rabbit's environment consistent, including the ambient temperature; sudden changes in temperature diminish a rabbit's natural resistance. A listless, unhappy, unhungry bunny requires your attention, as these are signs of pneumonia, in addition to mucus around the mouth and nasal passages. The assistance of a vet is essential, as most rabbits die within a few days of contracting the illness.

Sore hocks: Sore hocks are normally caused by insufficient bedding in the hutch. Tender, cracked and possibly scabbing skin covers the infected hind limb where the fur has been rubbed away. Since the smaller rabbits have larger foot padding on the hind feet, the larger breeds are more typically affected. Cleaning and applying an antiseptic ointment help the rabbit to recovery. Veterinary advice is also recommended.

Slobbers, Hutch burn and Scabby face: These three problems are serious and you should take your pet to the vet if you suspect that it has any of them. **Slobbers** is caused by abscesses of the mouth and the rabbit drools continuously. Little can be done for slobbers, and the affected animal will need to be put down. **Hutch burn**, commonly known as vent disease, is caused by dirt contacting the sex organ of the rabbit. The infected organ then becomes scabby and later purulent. Not surprisingly, infected rabbits exhibit a great reluctance to mate (which is fortunate for its partner, who could become contaminated). If the rabbit licks its infected private parts, a **scabby face** and mouth may result. A vet should be contacted as soon as possible.

Top: The Blue Dutch variety is one of the most popular pet rabbits.
Below: This Lop Eared rabbit has been allowed to roam outside but rabbits should not be left unsupervised.

BREEDING

If you are at all familiar with rabbits, then you are aware of their great capacity to reproduce. There have been litters as large as eighteen rabbits but relax - the average litter is about six. If you wish to raise a family of rabbits, keep in mind that doing so requires an investment of time and money on your part and, most importantly, consideration of what you will do with all the youngsters.

If you have two rabbits, the prospects of your having a little family are good, provided that you have a male and female. How do you tell if your rabbits are male or female rabbits? It is difficult to tell sometimes in rabbits that are less than eight to ten weeks of age. The process of determining the sex of an animal is called sexing. In some animals, such birds and snakes, sexing is almost impossible from simple

observation. Fortunately, sexing rabbits is pretty easy. Just look at the rabbit's private parts to tell whether it is male or female. Gently pull forward the skin directly in front of your furry friend's genitals and back from the tail end. If you have a male rabbit, his little penis will be visible, and maybe the testicles too; if you have a female rabbit, her slit-like organ, which is closer to the rear than the male's penis, will open up when pressure is exerted. Only a more experienced person can tell the sex of a very young rabbit. Generally, though, the male has a broader head and is somewhat smaller than the female. Unfortunately head shape is variable even within a litter, so this rule is not very reliable, even in adults.

A female rabbit, or doe, can be bred from as early as five months in the case of small breeds, but is better left until eight or nine months for giant breeds. Also, a doe should not be allowed more than three litters a year. If she is a healthy rabbit, she will be able to have babies until she is three or four years old. The gestation period of the rabbit is quite short: 30 to 32 days.

When you are ready to breed your rabbit, introduce the doe to the male, or buck, in the buck's cage. If they seem friendly, leave them undisturbed. Sometimes, a breeding is not successful on the first attempt; in this case, several visits from the doe may be necessary.

If you have any doubts about whether or not the mating has taken place, stop bringing the doe to the buck. Let a few days go by. Then bring the doe back to the buck's hutch. If she seems irritated or growls at him, it is quite likely that mating has already taken place. After mating, the doe becomes rather upset at further attention from the male.

The mother-to-be needs adequate rest and proper food during her pregnancy. Make life comfortable during this month. You may wish to offer a vitamin supplement.

Provide the doe with a nest box and nesting material about a week before the babies are due to be born. She will arrange the nest herself and will add to its warmth and comfort by padding it with bits of her own fur. During this time, do not

Two Orange Satins, a Silver Fox Satin and a Chinchilla Satin.

29

disturb the doe or the hutch, except for essentials such as feeding. Don't be concerned if she becomes increasingly nervous as the big day approaches.

The New Family

It is important that you do not disturb the doe or her babies. Try to restrain your curiosity, at least for the first five days. If you must take a peek, choose a time when the mother is out of the nest and make it a quick look. Make sure no light shines on the babies because, at this time, their eyes are highly sensitive. The doe knows by instinct how to raise her young and, if she is interfered with and someone tries to handle her babies, she may disown or even kill them. This may sound like strange behaviour from a mother who loves her children but it is not uncommon in the rabbit world. Your rabbit, no matter how fond she may be of you, is instinctively distrustful during this sensitive period.

Baby rabbits are born with their eyes closed and are hairless. In a few days, though, these little infants will have grown a soft protective fuzz and, in a couple of weeks, they will have developed a coat. By this time their eyes will be open and their ears perked up. After three weeks, the new bunnies will be hopping about on their own. As soon as they can do this, they will begin to feed themselves. During this period they should not be weaned; this comes later, at about five to eight weeks. Then, the youngsters may nibble on a good quality rabbit mix. Some hobbyists like to offer the young rabbits a vitamin supplement. If you give too much green food to rabbits, they may develop diarrhoea.

An example of a show-quality Chinchilla Giganta.

The Netherland Dwarf's good temperament makes it an ideal pet for a younger owner.

CONCLUSION

To own a rabbit is to love a rabbit. Playful, mischievous, and most entertaining, rabbits return the affection of children and grown-ups in a manner all their own. They are like no other pet. These furry little bundles are quiet - so quiet - yet active! They are never still for a moment. Noses quiver, legs thump, ears twitch. It's all symptomatic of the happy, well-housed and well-cared-for rabbit. Children love their long-eared friends on sight. They learn to care for them as they play with them. Responsibility is acquired in a simple, straightforward manner, and your children will be better for it. Many is the family that bought a rabbit or acquired one as a gift and then looked for a second. Rabbits are delightful to hold, handle, watch and enjoy. Rare indeed is the family that, having kept rabbits, now has them no more. Rabbits are so easy to care for, made of such sturdy stuff, and so enjoyable to have around that they have come to rival dogs and cats in popularity. They are relatively inexpensive to maintain. They take up little space. They are clean. And they are forever happy.

You have only to look into the bright eyes of a rabbit to love it. Stroke the fur and feel the beat of the heart and you won't want to let it go. The rabbit seems to have been created to be fondled and loved. Its lengthy ears search for your kind word, and the ever-twitching nose converses with you in rabbit language. It has been bred to be a pet, to receive and return affection. This it does most nobly.

As a proud and fond rabbit owner, you can extend your interest to the fascinating world of exhibition and other rabbit activities. Whether you live in Great Britain, North America or other parts of the world, there are national organisations that serve the rabbit community. Breed specialist clubs and membership organisations sponsor a variety of enjoyable events that typically are open to all rabbit fanciers, though perhaps not to all rabbit varieties. For more information, fanciers are encouraged to contact the British Rabbit Council, which can give you details of both local and national clubs and shows. Classes at shows often include 'care and condition', for crossbreeds and non-show-quality rabbits. The address is:

British Rabbit Council (BRC)
Purefoy House
7 Kirkgate
Newark
Notts
NG24 1AD

Getting together with other fanciers will make your hobby much more fun as you swap stories and experiences about your pet. And the rabbits like it too!

Be sure to supervise children with their rabbit friends.

BIBLIOGRAPHY

DWARF RABBITS
Gunter Flauhaus
ISBN: 0-86622-671-0
TFH (1990)

LOP RABBITS AS PETS
Sandy Crook
ISBN: 0-86622-137-9
TFH (1990)

THE PROPER CARE OF RABBITS
Darlene Campbell
ISBN: 0-86622-196-4
TFH (1995)

**CARE FOR YOUR RABBIT,
RSPCA GUIDE**
ISBN: 0-00412-546-0
Harper Collins (1996)

DWARF RABBITS, GETTING STARTED
Dennis Kelsey-Wood
ISBN: 0-86622-713-X
TFH (1997)

THE GUIDE TO OWNING A RABBIT
Anne Lindsay
ISBN: 0-79382-156-8
TFH (1997)

THE COMPLETE HOUSE RABBIT
Carolina James
ISBN: 1-85279-110-1
Kingdom (2000)

RABBITLOPAEDIA
Meg Brown and
Virginia Richardson MA VetMB MRCVS
ISBN: 1-86054-182-8
Ringpress (2000)

THE REALLY USEFUL BUNNY GUIDE
Carolina James
ISBN: 1-85279-033-4
Kingdom (1997)